JULIUS CAESAR
AND THE
ROMANS

Robin May

Illustrations by Gerry Wood

The Bookwright Press
New York · 1985

LIFE AND TIMES

Julius Caesar and the Romans
Alfred the Great and the Saxons

Further titles are in preparation

First published in the United States in 1985 by
The Bookwright Press, 387 Park Avenue South,
New York, NY 10016

First published in 1984 by
Wayland (Publishers) Ltd,
49 Lansdowne Place, Hove,
East Sussex BN3 1HF, England

ISBN 0–531–03823–8

Library of Congress Catalog Card Number 84-72075

Filmset in Monophoto Plantin by
Latimer Trend & Company Ltd, Plymouth
Printed in Italy by G. Canale & C.S.p.A., Turin

Contents

1 THE STORY OF CAESAR

Early life

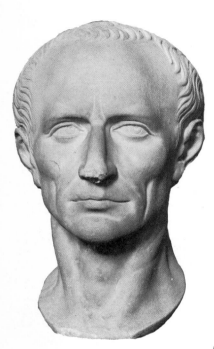

The head of Julius Caesar from a statue in the British Museum.

Within two years of his assassination in 44 B.C., Julius Caesar was declared a god. Divine or not, he was certainly a military genius and a great statesman. By the standards of his time he was not a brutal man, but he was certainly not merciful. As a young man in his twenties, he was captured by pirates, who demanded a ransom. While awaiting it, he played dice and joked with his captors. He told them that one day he would crucify them. He did.

Julius was born into a noble family about 102 B.C. His aunt Julia was married to the humbly born Marius, a general who led the popular party against the Senate, the aristocratic ruling council of state, and Caesar sided with him.

These were dangerous times. The great Republic, now the leading power of the ancient world, was going through a period of misgovernment by the nobility and was nearing civil war. How this came about we shall see later. The leading senator was Sulla, who had recently butchered some 3,000 of his opponents. When young Caesar married Cornelia, who had family connections with the Marius party, Sulla told him to divorce her—to test his loyalty. Thanks to some influential connections, he managed to get out of Rome alive. There was no divorce!

His military career began at this time in Asia, and when he returned to Rome after Sulla's death in 78 B.C., he was clearly a man with a bright future ahead of him.

Right *As a young man, Julius Caesar was captured by pirates and held for ransom.*

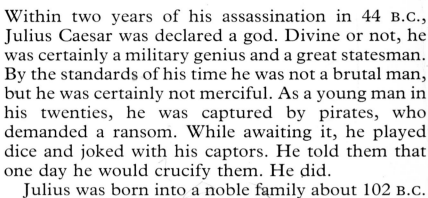

Politician and soldier

Back in Rome, Caesar plunged into public life. He showed ability in the law courts and in offices of state, and spent a great deal of money entertaining important people to gain their support in the future.

During this period, the leading member of the nobles' party was a brilliant general named Pompey, but he soon left Rome to make a great reputation fighting in Asia. In 60 B.C., Caesar became consul, meaning that he and one other would rule Rome for a year. To counter growing opposition, he teamed up with the richest man in Rome, Crassus—who paid his debts—and Pompey, now returned and converted to the popular party. They formed a "triumvirate"—a government of three.

Sensing trouble ahead, Caesar decided that an army behind him would be a sound investment. So, after giving Pompey his daughter in marriage—another sound move—he obtained the governorships of Cisalpine Gaul (north Italy), Illyricum to the east and untamed Transalpine Gaul (roughly modern France and Belgium).

From 58 to 50 B.C., he waged his Gallic Wars, also writing brilliantly about them. He had setbacks, and his two famous expeditions to "Britannia" were little more than reconnaissance trips, but in the end his triumph in Gaul was total. Rome had a great new province. His men adored him because he knew his job and looked after them well. He now had a mighty force behind him.

Below *Caesar used elaborate siege equipment in his attacks on enemy strongholds in Gaul.*

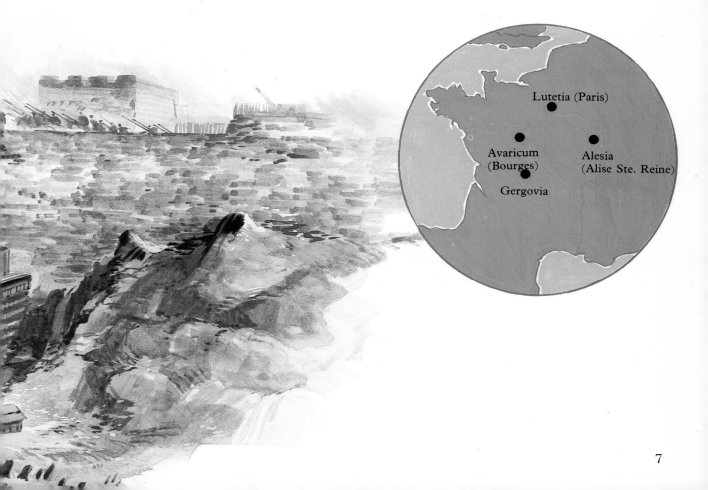

Master of Rome

Queen Cleopatra of Egypt. Caesar was bewitched by her for a time.

Caesar had given his country Gaul, but not everyone was pleased. Pompey no longer had family links with Caesar for his wife had died. He had now sided with the nobility, and urged the Senate to make Caesar disband his army and return to Rome.

Caesar headed south with his veterans, pausing at the small Rubicon River where his province ended. It would mean civil war if he crossed it, but cross it he did, and Rome welcomed him.

Pompey escaped to Greece, where Caesar defeated him at Pharsalus in 48 B.C. Again Pompey fled—to Egypt, where he was murdered. Caesar arrived to pardon him but instead was given his severed head!

Caesar stayed in Egypt for a time, bewitched by Cleopatra, whom he restored to the throne seized from her by her brother. Three years of widespread warfare followed until at last he was master of the Roman world and returned to Rome. He enjoyed spectacular triumphs for his great victories.

He was not vindictive to his enemies. He made plans to improve his country and to replace the misgovernment of the nobility with strong rule. But he was given such wide powers, including the position of dictator for life, that it seemed to many he would make himself king. A conspiracy was formed, some being true republicans such as Caesar's friend Brutus, while others were petty, jealous men. On the 15th of March 44 B.C., "the Ides of March," Caesar was assassinated at a Senate meeting. Perhaps ambition had clouded his judgment and made him forget the republican traditions of Rome. But he towered above his killers and he towers in history to this day.

Right *Caesar's body lies outside the Senate in Rome.*

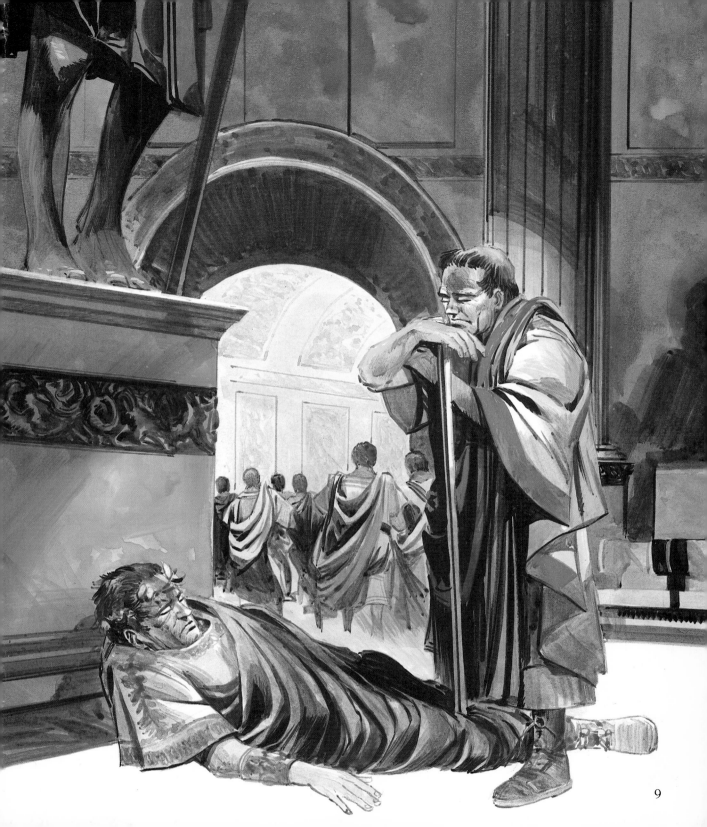

9

2 WHO WERE THE ROMANS?

Small beginnings

According to the ancient Romans, their city was founded by Romulus, son of the god Mars and a king's daughter, in 753 B.C. He and his brother Remus had been thrown into the Tiber River by a usurper, washed ashore and suckled by a she-wolf. Later, Romulus started to build Rome and Remus sneeringly jumped over the foundations. So Romulus killed him.

In fact, the first settlers came to Rome before 753 B.C., for archaeologists have found their remains on two of Rome's seven hills. The hills were easy to defend and there was a place where the Tiber could be crossed.

Peoples from the east had occupied the Italian peninsula from about 1500 B.C., no doubt swamping earlier inhabitants. However, the infant Rome was to be shaped by a still little-known people called the Etruscans, who came to Italy in about 700 B.C.

They were city dwellers and fine craftsworkers, using metal expertly and famed for their skill with gold. Their nobles were well educated and although they used the Greek alphabet, their language remains an almost total mystery. Etruscan kings ruled in a number of cities, one of them being Rome. From about 600 B.C., it was beginning to form its own identity as a Latin and Etruscan city. The Romans later invented many stories about this period, but hard facts are in short supply.

Above *A bronze statue of Romulus and Remus being suckled by a she-wolf.*

Below *Settlements in Italy in the sixth century* B.C.

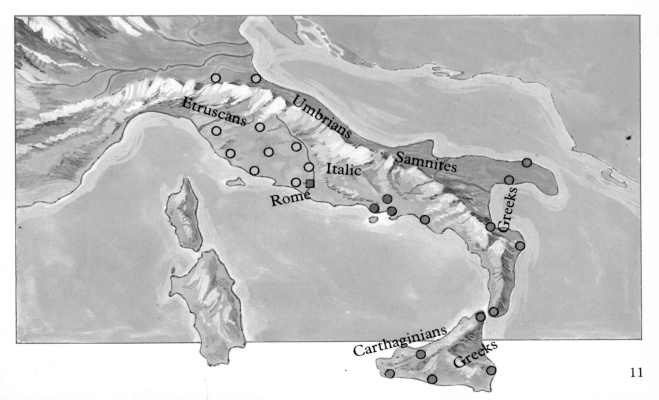

The Etruscans expelled

Before they were driven out, the Etruscan rulers of Rome laid the foundations of the powerful city it was to become. Under them, it became a real city. They drained some marshy ground with sewers and paved it, turning it into the political and religious heart of the city, the *Forum Romanum*. A great temple was built to the god Jupiter and the goddesses Minerva and Diana on the Capitoline Hill. The city's defenses were also strengthened.

Rome became a trading center, helped by the fact that ships could reach her up the Tiber River. And it was probably at this period that all property-owning citizens first had to do military service when the need arose. Not until the last century B.C. would Rome have a fully professional army.

All this was happening between 600 and 500 B.C. Legend has it that the Etruscan kings were thrown out of Rome in 510, and that is probably fairly correct. Etruscan power in central Italy was weakening generally and other cities were throwing off their yoke.

However, it seems that the Etruscans did attempt a comeback, and the great story of how Horatius and two comrades held the bridge over the Tiber, against an Etruscan army trying to put King Tarquin back on the throne, is not necessarily legend. Horatius finally held the bridge alone as it was cut down behind him, then he leapt into the Tiber and swam to safety. No one has yet proved it didn't happen!

Rome was now on its own.

A stone head of a warrior dating from the Etruscan period.

Left *The famous story of Horatius holding the bridge over the Tiber against the army of King Tarquin.*

13

3 THE RISE OF ROME
The young Republic

Now Rome was a republic and was to be one for some 450 years. The city was still small and was ruled by the Senate, to which only patricians—the nobles—could belong. The famous initials SPQR stood for "the Roman Senate and People," but the "plebs" (short for the plebeians—the ordinary people) had no real power as yet.

From the ranks of the Senate were elected two consuls each year, who were powerful in peace and war. The system, a deliberate change from all-powerful kings, worked well as a rule, but could fail badly in war if one or both men lacked military ability. Hannibal the Carthaginian (see page 21) was virtually unconquerable for many years, but on several occasions his task was made easier by this strange system.

In 494 B.C., the plebeians rebelled and the result was that the Senate allowed them to have two tribunes to speak up for them, and also their own assembly. Later, one consul had to be a plebeian.

A start was made on expanding the boundaries of Rome. No one at that time could have foreseen the mighty empire to come, and the expansion was not just for more land and power. Rome had many bitter rivals. There were setbacks. In 390 B.C., the Gauls attacked and sacked the city, the Capitol being saved, so one story has it, because its sacred geese created so much noise that the guards were alerted.

Rome usually allowed conquered cities self-government, but they naturally had to be loyal. To acquire Roman citizenship, people had to settle in Rome itself.

Below *The axe and fasces (bundles of sticks), were the symbols of a consul's power in ancient Rome.*

Mastering Italy

For many, the image projected by the word "Roman" is of a luxury-loving people, living in riches and splendor while the all-conquering legions added yet more territory to the Empire.

This image is totally wrong for the period when Rome was mastering Italy. Then the Romans were a stern, practical people, firmly believing in law and order and love of their country. Many were citizen farmers. As we shall see, these tough, patriotic people were even able to survive a series of catastrophic defeats by the great Hannibal.

Southern Italy came under control of the Romans in the 270s B.C. There were Greek colonies in the south and they called in King Pyrrhus of Epirus in Greece to help them against the Romans. He used elephants at the battle of Heraclea in 280 B.C., terrifying the Roman horses and no doubt the soldiers. But Pyrrhus lost so many of his own men that the phrase "Pyrrhic victory" came to mean victory won at excessive cost. After several more doubtful victories, he went home in 274 B.C. and southern Italy came under Roman domination.

Rome's conscript soldiers, all property owners, had to serve 16 years as infantrymen or 10 as cavalrymen in this period. Subject states and allies contributed their quota. Fortunately for the conscripts, war was then conducted only in spring and summer.

The spread of Roman power meant the spread of the Latin language of Rome. Ancient Latium bordered Rome and had been absorbed by the Romans by the third century B.C.

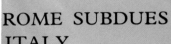

ROME SUBDUES ITALY

1	396 B.C.	Conquest of Veii
2	390 B.C.	Sack of Rome Gauls.
3	340 B.C.	Veseris—Latins subdued.
4	321 B.C.	Caudine Fork Samnites trap defeat a wh Roman army.
5	295 B.C.	Final victory o Samnites.
6	275 B.C.	Defeat of Pyrrh King of Epirus.
7	225 B.C.	Telamon—great feat of Gauls.

Cartha

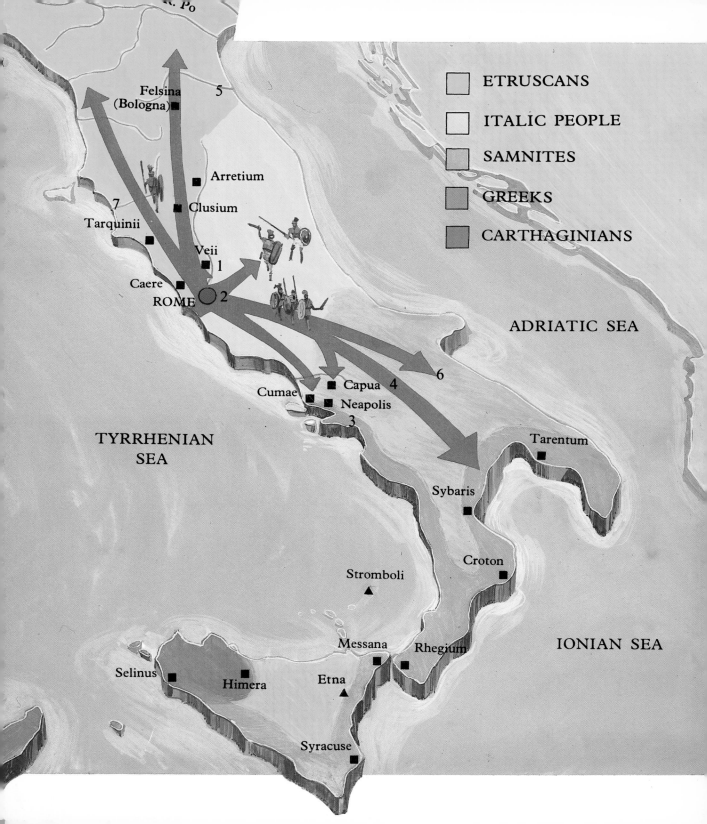

R. Po

Felsina
(Bologna)

5

Arretium

7

Clusium

Tarquinii

Veii

1

Caere

2

ROME

ETRUSCANS

ITALIC PEOPLE

SAMNITES

GREEKS

CARTHAGINIANS

ADRIATIC SEA

6

Cumae

Capua 4

Neapolis

3

TYRRHENIAN
SEA

Tarentum

Sybaris

Stromboli

Croton

Messana

Rhegium

IONIAN SEA

Selinus

Himera

Etna

Syracuse

4 ROME VERSUS CARTHAGE

The First Punic War

It took three wars to decide whether Rome or Carthage should rule the Mediterranean world. Carthage had been founded about 850 B.C. as a Phoenician colony. Phoenicia was where Lebanon is today. The Phoenicians were good seamen and born traders. They liked trade better than war and preferred hiring mercenaries to fight their battles. Carthage, like other Phoenician colonies, eventually became an independent state.

Below *A Roman galley—a decoration from a stone column in Rome.*

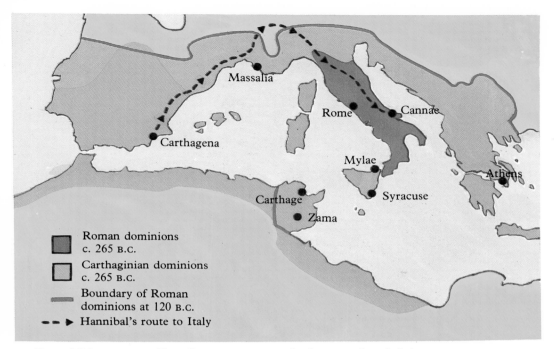

Roman dominions
c. 265 B.C.

Carthaginian dominions
c. 265 B.C.

Boundary of Roman
dominions at 120 B.C.

Hannibal's route to Italy

By 300 B.C., Carthage controled north Africa, western Sicily, southern Spain and the western Mediterranean. Inevitably, Rome and Carthage clashed—for the first time in 264 B.C. This was called the First Punic War, "Punic" coming from "Poeni"—Latin for Phoenicians.

Despite having no navy, Rome started the war, the prize being Sicily. The Romans built a strong fleet based on a storm-wrecked Carthaginian ship. They invented a mobile grappling plank with a spike at its end that could be swiveled and dropped on to an enemy deck, and they won their first naval victory in 260. Then they invaded Africa and Carthage gave in, but soon revolted because of the harsh terms.

The renewed war was fought in Sicily. Despite having lost her fleet for the third time in the war, Rome built another one and, finally, triumphed in 241 B.C. Sicily, Corsica, and Sardinia were hers; Carthaginian galleys were banned from Roman waters; and a huge sum was demanded from the citizens of Carthage. Another war was inevitable.

19

Carthage's revenge

Hamilcar the Carthaginian wanted revenge. He made his 9-year-old son Hannibal swear that he would never forget that Rome was Carthage's eternal enemy. The boy grew up to keep his oath and proved to be one of the greatest generals in history in a war—the Second Punic War—that was one of the greatest conflicts of the ancient world.

Hamilcar had built up Carthage's Spanish empire until it was a dagger pointing at Rome's heart, but Hamilcar was drowned before he could complete his work and his brilliant brother-in-law Hasdrubal was also killed. So 26-year-old Hannibal became his nation's avenger.

Already a great leader, and adored by his men, who came from every part of the western Mediterranean, Hannibal planned the impossible—an attack on Italy in late autumn via the Alps! With him went 50,000 men and 38 elephants from Africa and India. Crossing the Rhône River under attack from wild tribes was a remarkable achievement. Crossing the Alps in just 15 terror-filled days—under attack from more hostile tribes—was the greatest military feat of the ancient world.

Half of Hannibal's army survived, pouring down into Italy and winning three great victories, the greatest being at Cannae in 216 B.C.

The shaken but resolute Romans decided to avoid pitched battles and, instead, devastated areas to keep Hannibal short of supplies. He did not try to take the heavily fortified capital. He wanted to break the Roman will to fight. He kept Italy in a state of shock for twelve years.

Hannibal, the great Carthaginian general.

Left *Hannibal and his army cross the Alps on their way to Italy. Only one of the elephants is reputed to have survived the journey.*

Carthage totally destroyed

The position of the still-undefeated Hannibal steadily weakened. Rome and her allies could raise new armies; Hannibal had to find what troops he could. He got no support from Carthage, whose citizens were jealous of his fame and busy making fortunes. And Rome had at last found a great general, named Scipio, who admired and learned from Hannibal. It was Scipio who conquered Spain for Rome.

Below *Carthage was besieged for three years before being completely destroyed.*

In 203 B.C., Hannibal was recalled to Carthage to meet the threat from Scipio, now in Africa. The final battle was fought at Zama the next year. Scipio had some 43,000 trained troops; Hannibal about 50,000, mostly untrained, and 80 untrained elephants, which caused havoc to their own side. Scipio won one of the decisive battles of history, giving Rome mastery of the Mediterranean world.

The Carthaginians turned on Hannibal and he became a wanderer, for the Romans were out to get him. Finally, he poisoned himself.

Some Romans still feared even a powerless Carthage. Her people made her prosperous again despite a huge annual payment, but she had enemies in Rome. Worst was the statesman Cato who ended every speech on any subject with "Carthage must be destroyed!" An excuse was made for war and Carthage was besieged for three years, her people heroically making up for their past behavior. When Carthage fell in 146 B.C., the survivors were sold as slaves and the city was totally destroyed.

Scipio, the Roman general who at last defeated Hannibal.

23

5 THE GREAT REPUBLIC

Two years after Hannibal's defeat at Zama, Athens and other Greek cities asked Rome for help against Philip of Macedon to the north, who had sided with Carthage. The long-term result was a take-over of all Greece by 133 B.C. Fortunately for the Greeks, Rome was so in awe of their culture that they were ruled lightly by Rome—unless they misbehaved.

However, with the Republic soaring to new heights, success brought its problems. Much of Italy, especially the south, had been reduced to poverty by the Carthaginian wars. Rich men bought farms and had them run by chained gangs of slaves, while the impoverished farmers and peasants flocked to Rome, now colossally rich from all her conquests.

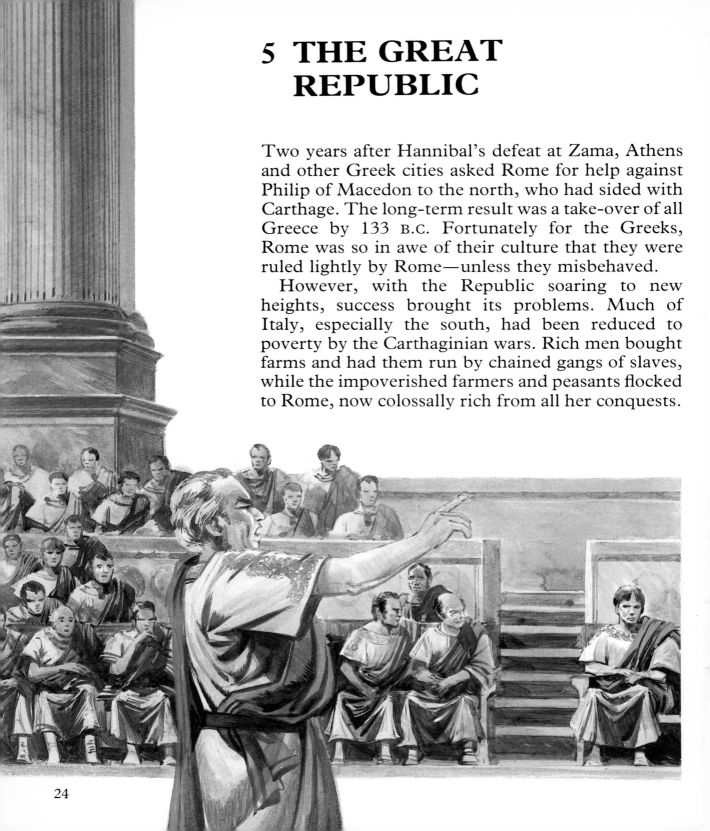

Instead of an army of property owners with a stake in Rome's future, the army became a professional force and a potential threat to the state in the hands of an ambitious general. Corruption was rife in the once honest capital, and with it went street violence and sometimes mass slaughter of political opponents. Slaves, not all of them unhappy (see page 36), were everywhere.

A century after Carthage was razed to the ground, the Roman Empire extended from Spain and Gaul to Syria and what is now western Turkey. In 44 B.C., Julius Caesar was murdered, as we saw on page 8. Fortunately, his adopted son, Augustus, was ready to save and transform Rome.

Left *The Roman Senate in action.*

Above *The Triumvirate that ruled Rome in 60 B.C. From left to right, Pompey, Caesar and Crassus.*

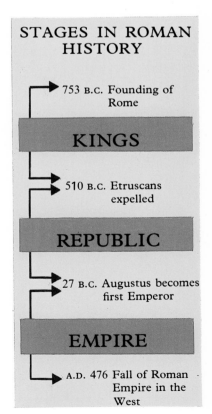

STAGES IN ROMAN HISTORY

753 B.C. Founding of Rome

KINGS

510 B.C. Etruscans expelled

REPUBLIC

27 B.C. Augustus becomes first Emperor

EMPIRE

A.D. 476 Fall of Roman Empire in the West

6 LIFE IN ANCIENT ROME

The teeming capital

About 1,800 years ago, the city of Rome was near the peak of its grandeur. Even today, we can get some idea of what it was like because of the magnificence of its remains. Yet life in the city was often chaotic. There were too many narrow, overcrowded streets winding their way through the city, constant traffic congestion, and overcrowded tenement buildings. Despite good underground sewers, sanitary conditions in the tenements were terrible, which made them a constant health hazard. If it had not been for the public baths (see page 28), things would have been even worse.

To offset the congestion, wheeled traffic was not allowed in the city for the ten hours after dawn. The result was very noisy nights, especially for the poor in their overcrowded dwellings, as carts trundled by and curses and yells filled the air.

Naturally, fires were a constant hazard and houses frequently collapsed. Despite laws forbidding it, tenements were built higher and higher with wooden additions. When there was a fire, it was impossible to get water up in time. It needed no Christians to burn down Rome, as the Emperor Nero alleged they had. Fires were inevitable.

Thanks to Roman engineering skills, there was good drinking water to be had, transported into the city by great aqueducts from springs in the hills around the capital. Many of these aqueducts are still standing today.

Left *Splendid marble buildings dominated the center of ancient Rome.*

Baths for all

The Romans were a notably clean people. So were the Greeks before them who, like the Romans, made public baths an important feature of town life. People visited the local baths several times a week. They were popular meeting places not only in Rome but across the Empire. It was not just the bathing, though that took a long time, with hot and cold dips, dry heat, massages, etc. There were often gardens for a stroll and a chat, and shops to be visited. You could also get your hair cut and have a good meal.

The afternoon was the great time to visit the baths, below which were water storage cisterns. Furnaces of wood heated the water which came from

the city's aqueducts. Some, like those at Bath in England, used water from medicinal springs.

The bathers used olive oil to clean themselves, then scraped themselves with an implement to remove the oil and the sweat. As today, fitness enthusiasts believed in finishing off with a cold bath—in the *frigidarium*.

The baths were a particular boon to the poor, whose tenement buildings, as we have seen, were unsanitary and, indeed, without any water supply.

Meanwhile, the rich had baths in their own town and country houses and all over the Empire. Some bathers went in for special refinements. The Emperor Nero's wife Poppea, whom he is said to have kicked to death, used to bathe in asses' milk.

Above *The remains of the Roman baths today, in the city of Bath in southwest England.*

Going to school

Roman children of all classes, slaves included, seem to have been able to read and write, and this was true not just in the capital but in most parts of the Empire. Though some children of rich families had private tutors, many went to school. Wealthy parents often helped to start schools in their own towns.

In general, the schoolmaster was an honored citizen, though this was not the view shared by the great satirist Juvenal. He claims that even the most successful teacher never got a proper reward, that parents expected him to meet impossibly high standards, that he had to be a father to his charges—and that he earned less in a year than a successful jockey could win in a single race!

Mathematics was an important subject, for financial affairs played an important part in the Roman

world. A nobleman's son would also be expected to know his Greek and Latin literature, to study philosophy and—because he would be going into politics—rhetoric, the art of speaking impressively and persuasively in public. Rhetoric also included writing effectively.

Books were readily available to all, but as there was no printing press, all had to be copied by hand.

Girls too were educated and also studied what we would call domestic science, but many got married very young, which must have halted their full-time education. The fall of the Empire meant the end of a great age of learning.

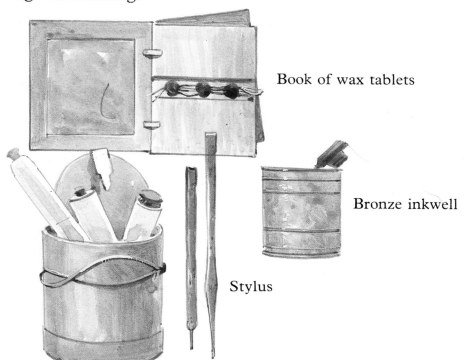

Book of wax tablets

Bronze inkwell

Stylus

Country life

Besides their houses in Rome, many wealthy families had villas in the country. The climate was good, the land fertile; but even in less pleasant climates the Romans liked country life. The remains of many Roman villas in Britain prove it.

With more space than in Rome, many of these villas were very grand indeed, with a central garden complete with columns. As is true today, much of the land around the villa was farmed, and villas were the center of country life in the area. Most were farms as well as dwellings.

These farms were run for profit, and an owner did his best to secure an honest and efficient manager to run his farm. Vine growing was very popular because it brought in a good profit, and sports included boar and deer hunting.

Many simply used the country to relax after a hard spell in the capital, and many villas overlooked the sea. The Bay of Naples, then as now, was a much sought after coastline.

We have seen how country life changed when peasants flocked to Rome, leaving farms to be run by chain gangs. Yet many Romans still enjoyed life outside the capital—and outside Italy. And travel was easy because of the magnificent roads that spanned the Roman world, as straight as possible, some 5 meters (15ft) across and excellently maintained.

Right *A Roman country villa. Many of these were run as large farms.*

Hand quern
(for grinding cor

32

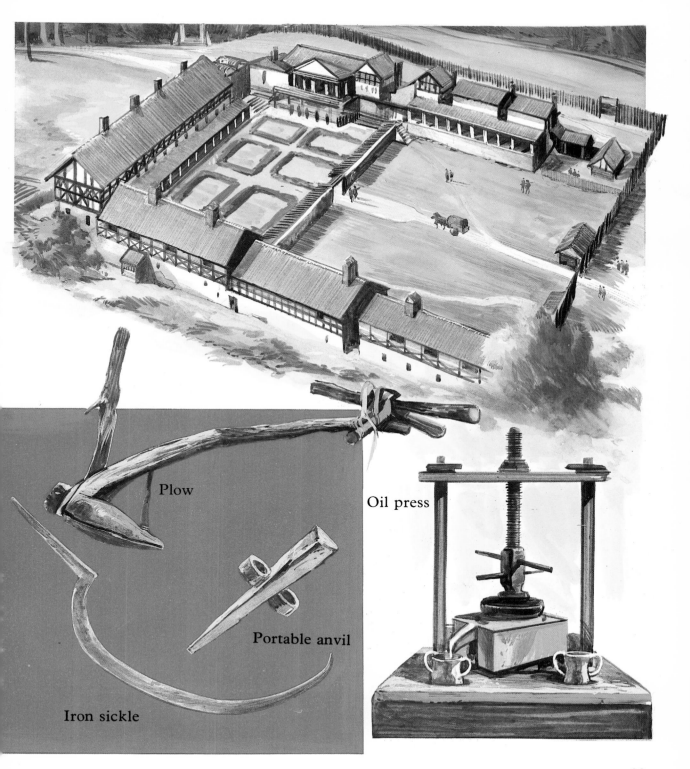

Plow

Oil press

Portable anvil

Iron sickle

Sports and slaughter

Rome's rulers had to feed and entertain the people most of whom were poor and jobless because of the number of slaves employed by the rich. In the first century A.D. there were over 150 public holidays a year, more than 90 being devoted to "games" paid for by the state.

Chariot races were held in Rome at the Circus Maximus, said to have held over 250,000 spectators. These were thrilling events, which could turn a humbly born charioteer, perhaps a slave, into a superstar.

There was also the theater. Roman theaters were big, open-air structures providing popular entertainment, but their plays were well below the standard of those of ancient Greece.

Shamefully popular was the Amphitheater. Romans of all classes flocked to the "entertainments" offered in Rome and across the Empire. Our century has seen enough horrors, but not in the name of show business. Least ghastly were gladiatorial combats, with gladiators fighting each other to the death, often with swords, sometimes with a net to entangle an opponent before killing him with a trident. There were many variations. A fallen gladiator who had fought well could be reprieved by the crowd; a successful one might become a popular hero. Most were slaves or prisoners.

Far worse were the mass slaughters in the great Colosseum at Rome and elsewhere in which men and women were torn to pieces by animals. These and other atrocities continued until the triumph of Christianity put an end to such spectacles.

Below *A highly decorated gladiator's helmet. An iron grill protected the face.*

Slaves and slavery

Above *Slaves carrying their master through the street on a litter.*

Given that slavery is always evil, the fact remains that many slaves in ancient Rome led a much better life than poor freemen. In rich households, the doctor and the schoolmaster might be Greek slaves, and it was common sense to treat household slaves well. Slaves got some pay, and some day they might be allowed to buy their freedom—or be granted it.

Of course, there were many bad slave-masters, but the life of the average slave in Rome cannot be compared to that of the misery of those working in chain gangs on farms. They were chained night and day and lived underground.

Below *This Roman stone decoration shows a Roman household in action. The master of the house is seated at top center, while all around him slaves are preparing food and drink.*

The Emperor Augustus had a bodyguard of slaves. Crassus, Julius Caesar's rich friend, had a fire brigade of slaves and used to accompany them to fires and put in bids for the burning properties!

Rome's huge conquests increased the supply of slaves. By Trajan's reign (A.D. 98–117), it has been estimated that there were some 1,200,000 free Romans and 400,000 slaves.

Naturally, Christianity appealed to slaves with its doctrine that all men were equal. There were many slave uprisings. The most famous was led by Spartacus, a gladiator, from 73 to 71 B.C. He defeated Roman armies with runaway slaves in a civil war that was ended by Crassus. As a grisly example to the rest, those captured were crucified along the road from Rome to the south, called the Appian Way.

Above *A slave helps his master to adjust his toga.*

Below *Many slaves were crucified following the great slave revolt of Spartacus.*

Above *Vestal Virgins performing religious rites in the temple of Vesta.*

Roman religion

The early Roman peasant farmers and their neighbors in Latium believed in spirits called *numina*, which controled people's lives. They were worshipped with prayers and offerings. Every key aspect of life had its *numen* (the singular of *numina*). Vesta guarded the home's fire and hearth; Janus guarded the door and other household gods were called *lares* and *penates*. The *lar familiaris* was the spirit of the founder of the house, and the *lares* as a whole were heroes or ancestors who had become gods.

The *penates* were gods of the storeroom and of the household—and also of the state. There was a shrine to them in every house and offerings of incense, wine and food were made to them on special occasions. Offerings were made to the spirits of the dead and gods of the underworld, while there were special festivals to guarantee a good harvest.

These gods and festivals became the basis of the state religion. However, the Romans were always willing to absorb other gods, including the Greek ones. For instance the supreme god Jupiter (Jove) corresponded to the Greek deity Zeus.

When the Roman state became a huge empire, Romans became less religious. Many looked towards Middle Eastern cults which preached an afterlife and salvation. These helped pave the way for Christianity, a persecuted cult in the first century A.D., but the state religion by the end of the fourth century.

Above *Jupiter was the supreme Roman god.*

Below *In the early centuries of persecution, Christians practiced their religion in secret, in underground tombs called the Catacombs on the outskirts of Rome.*

The Roman army

Rome's greatness as a world power was due more to her army than to anything else. The key to its success was the legion, which at the most was 6,000 strong, and the key members of a legion were the centurions. These were officers who were renowned for their trustworthiness and valor.

Most of the legion were infantrymen, with some cavalry. The Romans also used auxiliary troops, who were non-citizens, raised in the provinces.

A legion also had road- and bridge-building

specialists. Every evening, while in hostile territory, the legionaries set up a defensive camp, complete with trenches and ramparts. This was called a *castra*. British towns with "chester" or "caster" in their names were once Roman camps.

The centurions and their men were usually victorious given reasonable leadership. We have seen how Rome changed to a professional army in the first century B.C. This had its disadvantages, for troops now gave allegiance to their generals rather than the state, a recipe for civil war in some cases.

Yet the Roman army, despite occasional disasters against cavalry and guerrillas, remained a unique force for 700 years. Even against Hannibal, it kept renewing itself. Meanwhile, the retired soldier could expect a pension or land in the provinces.

As we shall see, mounted barbarians were finally incorporated into the legions to fight other invading barbarians. Then, Rome and its legions crumbled.

Above *Roman soldiers used their shields to form an attacking formation called a "tortoise."*

Below *A roman sword and dagger.*

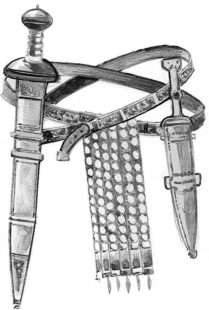

Left *Roman soldiers from a stone decoration.*

7 THE EMPIRE OF AUGUSTUS

Augustus and Antony

After Julius Caesar's murder, a ferocious power struggle erupted, affecting the whole Roman world. Mark Antony, a pleasure-loving soldier and henchman of Caesar's, made a speech at his funeral that turned the people against the assassins. He already had the army on his side.

Suddenly, Octavian, Caesar's 18-year-old great-nephew and heir, came forward just as Antony was making himself master of Rome. No one had yet touched the assassins, and Caesar's troops urged his heir to destroy them, but first the clever youth told the Romans about the fortune that his great-uncle had left them. Under pressure to destroy Antony's ambitions, he bided his time, forming a second triumvirate with him and a nobody called Lepidus. They savagely purged their enemies.

Next, the killers of Caesar were defeated at Philippi in Greece. Then Antony went to Egypt, there to begin his legendary love affair with Cleopatra. Octavian returned to Rome.

Aided by a brilliant general and admiral named Agrippa, he now routed his enemies on land and sea. Meanwhile, his rival Antony was enjoying himself at the Egyptian court. He gave Roman territory to Cleopatra, now his queen, and Octavian warned Rome that Antony wanted to give Rome an oriental-style monarchy. Finally, with Rome's approval, Octavian defeated Antony at the great sea battle of Actium in 31 B.C. The lovers committed suicide, and Octavian became Rome's first emperor—Augustus.

The Emperor Augustus.

Left and **Below** *Antony and Cleopatra were defeated by Octavian at the great sea battle of Actium—fought off the coast of Greece.*

The first emperor

Octavian, now called Augustus, played down his title. Power was in his hands and he was elected consul for a number of years, later taking consular power for life. He liked to be regarded as a *princeps* or chief—the chief citizen of Rome.

The soldiers—many of them veterans of Julius Caesar's armies—were completely loyal to him; the people, after the bitter civil wars, wanted peace; the nobility—what was left of it after the bloodbaths—resented him, but could only attack him with words.

Augustus formed the Praetorian Guard to serve him in Rome. He reduced the number of legions from 60 to 28, but was able to pay off those not

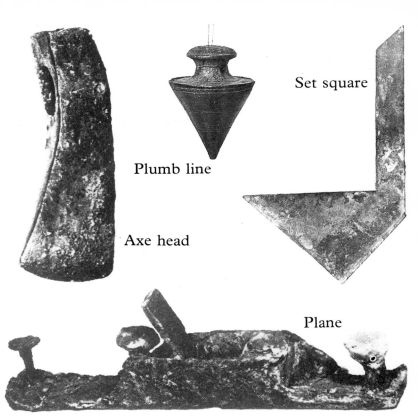

needed very handsomely from money taken from Egypt, which became his private treasure chest. He improved the quality of senators—Antony had let in some of his friends—but power remained firmly in his hands. He built temples and much else in Rome. Inefficient officials were weeded out. He wanted good administrators, responsible only to him.

This great Roman ruler—that he owed much of his success to the work of his great-uncle, Julius Caesar, does not lessen his greatness—inspired a revival of the old Roman patriotism. To it was added a sense of Rome's mission as an imperial power. The poet Virgil reveals this in his famous poem, *The Aeneid*; while Livy shows in his history of the Republic the same love of country. The "Augustan Age" was a glorious one.

8 MASTERS OF THE WORLD

Strengthening the borders

Fortunately for Rome, Augustus reigned for 45 years, dying in A.D. 14. His reign was the start of 200 years of peace for those within the Empire. He gave the Roman world *Pax Romana*—the Roman Peace.

Rome's Empire was pushed to its final bounds by the great Trajan, who ruled from A.D. 98 to 117. He conquered Dacia (modern Romania) and extended Rome's Asian Empire to its farthest limits. And limits there were, as a terrible disaster in A.D. 9 had proved. Barbarian hordes were always poised on the frontiers, kept at bay by the legions. Fortunately for Rome, the Rhine and the Danube—which rise near each other—formed a fine barrier against the fierce Germanic tribes. But Augustus decided to push forward from the Rhine to the Elbe to create an Elbe–Danube frontier.

In A.D. 9, a chief of the Cherusci tribe, named Arminius, surprised and totally destroyed three legions under Quinctilius Varus. When Augustus, now an old man, heard the appalling news, he beat his head against a door. For the rest of his life, he was liable to cry: "Varus, give me back my legions!" But the Romans learned their lesson. They resumed the Rhine–Danube frontier.

Within the Empire, commerce and industry flourished. The Mediterranean was full of ships carrying grain and other cargoes. When Augustus died, the whole Mediterranean world was a single nation.

Right *The Roman Empire at the time of its greatest extent under the Emperor Trajan.*

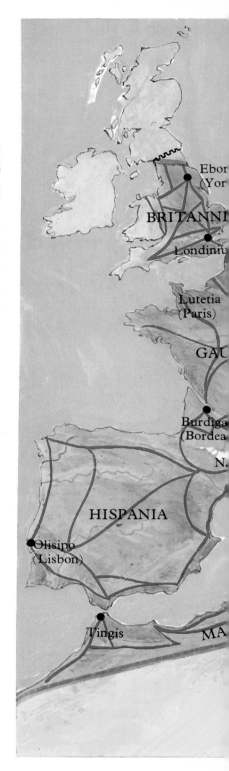

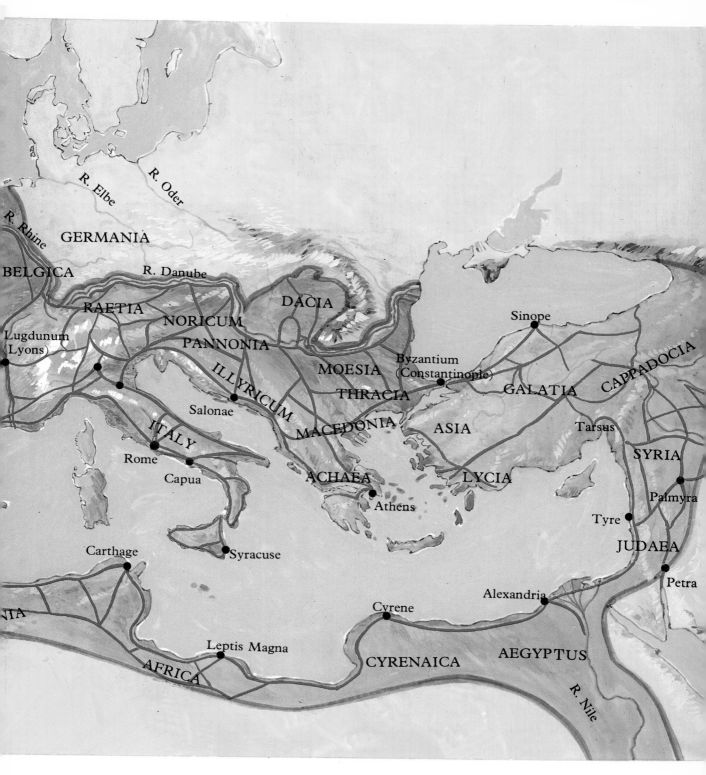

GERMANIA

R. Elbe

R. Oder

R. Rhine

BELGICA

R. Danube

RAETIA

NORICUM

PANNONIA

DACIA

Lugdunum
(Lyons)

ILLYRICUM

Salonae

MOESIA

THRACIA

Byzantium
(Constantinople)

Sinope

CAPPADOCIA

GALATIA

ITALY

Rome

Capua

MACEDONIA

ASIA

Tarsus

SYRIA

ACHAEA

LYCIA

Palmyra

Athens

Tyre

JUDAEA

Carthage

Syracuse

Petra

NIA

Alexandria

Cyrene

Leptis Magna

CYRENAICA

AEGYPTUS

AFRICA

R. Nile

47

Good and bad emperors

Below *To the northwest, the Roman Empire reached as far as Hadrian's Wall in the north of England.*

So strong was the machinery of state that Augustus set up, that the Empire survived a weird assortment of emperors. His stepson Tiberius succeeded him. A fine soldier, he became a sound ruler, but as his financial economies included cutting down on public games, the Romans hated him! Finally, he retired to the island of Capri, where he seems to have gone mad. He may have been murdered.

His great-nephew Caligula succeeded him in A.D. 37. He went insane, possibly through illness. Viciously cruel, Caligula insulted all and sundry by making his horse a priest and a consul!

Murdered in 41, he was succeeded by Claudius, Tiberius's nephew. Reviled by his enemies, Claudius was, it seems, an able ruler. He picked the wrong wives, however, the last of whom murdered him. Under him, Britain became part of the Empire. His successor Nero, his stepson, is best remembered for persecuting Christians. Nero killed his mother and wife, but did not burn down Rome as his enemies alleged. The last of the Augustan line, he killed himself to escape being murdered.

That was in A.D. 68 and civil war broke out. Four emperors were elected in a year; the last, a fine soldier named Vespasian, ended the chaos. Chosen by the army in the east, he left his son Titus to finish a bitter war against the Jews which ended when Jerusalem fell after a terrible siege in A.D. 70. Back in Rome, chaos gave way to peace and prosperity.

49

9 DECLINE AND FALL
A divided Empire

Above *The Emperor Trajan.*

Below *The Emperor Constantine plans a Christian church in his new city of Constantinople.*

Vespasian's line ended in A.D. 96 when his son Domitian, who had become more and more despotic, was murdered. A senator called Nerva became emperor and decided that the adoption of a successor was the best way to achieve good government. Augustus had hoped to achieve the same thing: this time it really worked. There was a century of fine government under the five "good" emperors—Nerva, Trajan, Hadrian, Antoninus Pius and the scholarly Marcus Aurelius. Only Nerva was Italian born, three being Spanish and one from Gaul.

The rot started again in A.D. 192 with the murder of Marcus Aurelius's horrible son Commodus. In 193, there were five claimants to the imperial throne, and in the century that followed there were constant attacks by barbarians across the Rhine and Danube.

In A.D. 286, the great Diocletian divided the Empire into East and West, himself ruling the East from Nicodemia in Asia Minor (modern Turkey) and Maximian ruling the West from Milan. So swollen was the Empire now that this seemed the best way of administering and protecting it, though the expense was colossal.

Later, the emperor Constantine reversed Diocletian's policy of persecuting Christians and finally made Christianity the Empire's official religion, though he was only baptized on his deathbed in A.D. 337. He made Byzantium the Eastern Empire's capital, calling it Constantinople. This Christian capital survived 1,000 years. Rome's days were numbered.

Above *Statue of Constantine.*

The sack of Rome

While Constantinople was growing in splendor, the Roman Empire in the West was declining fast. Towns were decaying and there was not enough money available to keep the army up to strength—in fact, its ranks consisted mainly of barbarian troops.

The crisis broke late in the fourth century when the Germanic people struck across Europe—the Goths assailing the Balkans while Saxons, Angles, and Jutes attacked Britain. Behind the Goths came a ferocious Asiatic people called the Huns; while other

invaders included the Vandals, and the Lombards and Burgundians. Whole peoples were on the move.

The next century was worse, the desperate Romans hiring more barbarians to keep out barbarians. The terrible Attila the Hun was now in action, while the Vandals invaded Africa through Spain, cutting Rome off from her main grain supply.

In A.D. 410 Rome herself was sacked by Goths; in 455 Vandals crossed the Mediterranean to sack her. Yet barbarians helped save the last shreds of Empire at Troyes in 451, when the Huns were driven out by a barbarian Roman army. But the end came in A.D. 476 when the German Odoacer deposed the last Roman emperor in the West.

Yet many of these barbarians were half Romanized. The remains of Rome's greatness were all around them. They strode along her roads. Many became Christians. Not for nothing is Rome called the Eternal City.

Left *Barbarian hordes pour into Rome.*

10 THE LEGACY OF ROME

Ancient Rome had fallen, yet she lived on and does so to this day. Many nations still use Roman law; while the Roman Catholic Church, which finally conquered the Roman world and which did much to lessen the fury of the barbarians, spans much of today's world.

Many languages are based on Latin; some, like English, are partly based on it. Roman literature is still studied and loved; Roman remains still thrill and inspire mankind. And the Romans did much to ensure the survival of the civilization of the Greeks that they so admired. Our calendar is based on the Julian calendar of Julius Caesar. Many of today's great cities, including London, date from Roman times, yet the whole amazing civilization had virtually started in a small hill town.

How could such a spot rise to such grandeur and greatness? Great it was despite all its faults, despite the nightmare of the blood-drenched arenas, the terrible acts of revenge on slaves who rebelled, and the purges of political rivals. This book has shown some of the reasons—Rome's position, the Etruscan influence, and other factors—but most important of all was the character of the early Romans, the resolution and courage that finally defeated Hannibal, the high quality of so many leaders. Yet the story still seems little short of a miracle.

Left *The legacy of Rome includes Roman law, architecture, coinage and language.*

Table of dates

New words

Amphitheater A round or oval building with rows of seats rising from an open central space, called an arena. It was the scene of gladiatorial fights and great slaughters.

Capitol Short form of Capitoline—the most important of the Seven Hills of Rome.

Circus Stadium where chariot races took place.

Forum The most important public place in a Roman city. It was part market place, part business center, part legal and debating center.

Gaul Consisted roughly of France and Belgium, plus parts of Germany, Holland and Switzerland.

Gladiators Swordsmen who fought to the death for the entertainment of the Romans. From the Latin word *gladius* meaning sword.

Lares Ancestral gods of a household.

Mars The Roman god of war.

Patricians Name given to the ancient nobility of Rome.

Penates Gods of the storeroom of a Roman's house, and of his household.

Plebeians The freemen and citizens of Rome who were not from the ancient noble families.

Province A division of the Roman Empire. Britain started as a single province, but by the reign of Diocletian it had been divided into four.

Tribune A powerful official. Two tribunes were first elected in 494 B.C. to protect the interests of the Plebs against the Patricians.

Triumph A procession to the Capitol in Rome in honor of a victorious general.

Trident A three-pronged spear used by gladiators in combat.

Consul Chief magistrates of Rome. Two were elected from the Senate each year and were powerful in peace and war.

Senate. The council of state in Rome, made up of the most important families. Its power was diminished during the Empire.

Picture Acknowledgments

Black and white photographs by the Mansell collection 5, 8, 11, 13, 15, 18, 21, 23, 31, 36, 39, 41, 43, 45, 49, 51; Wayland Picture Library 29, 50.

For further reading

Amery and Vanage. *Rome and Romans.* Tulsa, OK: Usborne/Hayes, 1976.

Andrews, Ian. *Pompeii.* Minneapolis, MN: Lerner, 1980.

Body, Hugh. *Roman People.* North Pomfret, VT: David & Charles, 1981.

Cairns, Trevor, ed. *The Romans and their Empire.* Minneapolis, MN: Lerner, 1974.

Chisolm, Jan. *Roman Times.* Tulsa, OK: EDC, 1982.

Church, Alfred J. *Roman Life in the Days of Cicero.* Totowa, NJ: Littlefield, Adams.

Forman, Joan and Strongman, Harry. *The Romans.* Morristown, NJ: Silver Burdett, 1977.

Hamey, L. A. *Roman Engineers.* Minneapolis, MN: Lerner, 1982.

Hamilton, Edith. *The Roman Way.* New York: Avon, 1973.

Peach, L. Dugarde. *Julius Caesar and Roman Britain.* Bedford Hills, NY: Merry Thoughts, 1968.

Purdy, Susan and Sandak, Cass R. *Ancient Rome.* New York: Franklin Watts, 1982.

Wilkes, John. *The Roman Army.* Minneapolis, MN: Lerner, 1977.

Index